D0773499

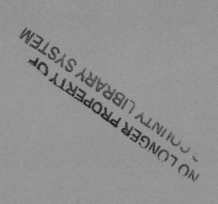

Lives and Times

Johann Sebastian Bach

Peggy Pancella

Heinemann Library
Chicago, Illinois

Designed by Lucy Owen and Bridge Creative Services
Originated by Modern Age Repro
Printed and bound by South China Printing Company

10 09 08 07 06
10 9 8 7 6 5 4 3 2 1

Library of Congress Cataloging-in-Publication Data
Pancella, Peggy.
  Johann Sebastian Bach / Peggy Pancella.
    p. cm. -- (Lives and times)
  Includes bibliographical references (p.   ) and index.
  ISBN 1-4034-6745-5 (library binding - hardcover)
  1. Bach, Johann Sebastian, 1685-1750--Juvenile
literature. 2. Composers--Germany--Biography--
Juvenile literature. I. Title. II. Series: Lives and times
(Des Plaines, Ill.)
  ML3930.B2P32 2005
  780'.92--dc22

                              2005004198

Acknowledgments
The author and publishers are grateful to the following
for permission to reproduce copyright material:
AKG-Images pp. **18, 23, 24, 25**; AKG-Images/Yale
University, Library of the School of Music p. **13**;
Alamy/Lebrecht Music and Arts Photo Library pp. **6, 11**;
Art Directors and Trip p. **27**; Corbis/Adam Woolfitt p. **5**;
Corbis/Archivo Iconografico, S.A. pp. **4, 26**;
Corbis/Richard Hamilton Smith p. **17**; Getty
Images/Photodisc p. **8**; Sally Barton pp. **9, 12, 21**; The
Art Archive/Bach House Leipzig/Dagli Orti (A) p. **20**;
The Art Archive/Bach House Eisenach/Dagli Orti (A)
p. **15**; The Art Archive/Mozart Museum Villa
Bertramka Prague/Dagli Orti (A) p. **10**; The Art
Archive/Museo Bibliografico Musicale Bologna/Dagli
Orti (A) p. **19**; The Bridgeman Art Library/
Kurpfalzisches Museum, Heidelberg, Germany,
Lauros/Giraudon p. **22**; The Bridgeman Art
Library/Heimatmuseum, Kothen, Germany p. **16**;
The Bridgeman Art Library/Schlossmuseum, Weimar,
Germany p. **14**; The Bridgeman Art Library/
Staatsbibliothek, Berlin, Germany p. **7**.

Cover picture of Johann Sebastian Bach reproduced
with permission of Bridgeman Art Library. Photograph
of music manuscript reproduced with permission of
Corbis.

Page icons by Corbis

Photo research by Maria Joannou and Virginia
Stroud-Lewis

Every effort has been made to contact copyright
holders of any material reproduced in this book.
Any omissions will be rectified in subsequent
printings if notice is given to the publishers.

Contents

Some words are shown in bold, **like this**. You can find out what they mean by looking in the glossary.

Introducing Johann Sebastian Bach

Johann Sebastian Bach loved music. He sang, played, and taught music. Most of all he wrote music. Today he is known as one of the greatest **composers** ever.

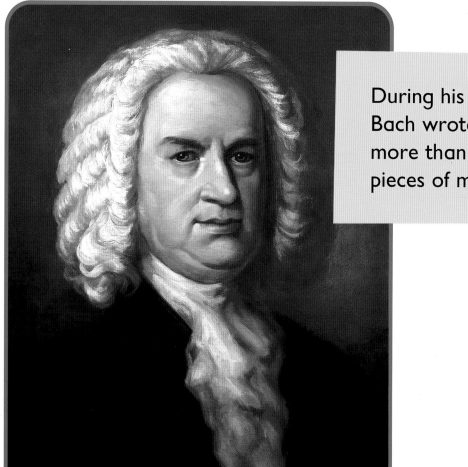

During his life Bach wrote more than 1,200 pieces of music.

This building is an example of the Baroque style.

Bach lived during a time called the **Baroque period**. People made artworks and buildings that were very fancy and beautiful. Bach wrote much of his music in this same grand **style**.

A Musical Family

Johann Sebastian Bach was born in Germany on March 21, 1685. He was the youngest of eight children. All of his brothers were named "Johann." They used their middle names instead.

The house where Sebastian was born is now a museum.

Sebastian grew up with music all around him. His father, grandfather, brothers, uncles, and cousins all played instruments. They met each year to play music together. They also made up new songs.

Sebastian's father played the violin and many other instruments.

Early Learning

Sebastian's father taught him to play the violin and **viola**. Later Sebastian went to school and sang in the church **choir**. But when he was only nine years old, both of his parents died.

Sebastian learned to play the violin when he was very young.

Sebastian spent hours learning music and writing new pieces.

Sebastian went to live with his oldest brother, Christoph. Christoph taught him to play the **organ** and **harpsichord**. Sebastian learned very quickly. He also started to **compose** his own music.

On His Own

When Sebastian was fifteen, his brother could no longer care for him. But Sebastian found a school that would let him stay and study for free. He and a friend walked for many days to get there.

Sebastian's fingers flew fast when he played **keyboard** instruments like this harpsichord.

Sebastian began his job as organist at this church when he was only eighteen years old.

Sebastian worked hard and got good grades. He sang in the **choir** and played the **organ** and **harpsichord**. When he finished school, he found work as a church **organist**.

11

Life Changes

Sebastian worked hard at his job, but things did not go well. People thought his playing was too fancy. They said his music was too hard to sing. Many of the singers did not get along with him.

Sebastian could play the hardest music without making mistakes.

Clavier - Büchlein.

von

Wilhelm Friedemann Bach.

angefangen in

Cöthen den

22. Januar

Ao. 1720.

This is the cover of some music that Sebastian wrote for his oldest son.

Sebastian soon quit his job. He found work at another church. In 1707 he married his cousin Maria Barbara. They had seven children, but three of them died young.

Court Musician

Sebastian's new job did not work out. The pay was low, and the church's **pastor** did not like fancy music. Soon a **duke** asked Sebastian to be his **court organist**. Sebastian quickly agreed.

Duke Wilhelm Ernst was one of Sebastian's first **patrons**.

Sebastian stayed with the duke for more than nine years. He **composed** many famous pieces. When Sebastian got a new job, the duke did not want him to go.

Sebastian wrote much of his best music while working at the duke's court.

Fürstl. Weimarische Residentz

Working for a Prince

Sebastian was happy with his new job. He worked for a prince who loved music. Prince Leopold liked Sebastian, too. He let Sebastian's family live in his palace.

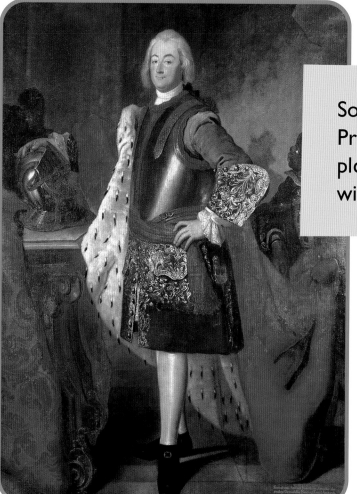

Sometimes Prince Leopold played music with Sebastian.

Orchestras today still play many of the pieces Sebastian **composed** during this time.

Sebastian had written a lot of music for the **organ**. Now he tried different kinds of music. Some of his new pieces were for many instruments to play together.

Sebastian's Growing Family

In 1720 Sebastian got some sad news. His wife had died while he was away on a trip. Soon he met a singer named Anna Magdalena. They married in 1721.

Sebastian's family spent many evenings making music together.

Four of Sebastian's sons grew up to be famous **musicians** and **composers**, including Johann Christian.

Sebastian and Anna Magdalena had thirteen children. Seven of them died young. Sebastian taught most of his children to play instruments. He wrote music for them to practice.

Different Styles of Music

Prince Leopold had also married, but his wife did not like music. So Sebastian left for the city of Leipzig. He made music for four churches and for town events. He also taught music at school.

Sebastian spent the rest of his life at St. Thomas's Church in Leipzig.

Sebastian **composed** huge pieces for singers and instruments. Some people said this music was too fancy for church. So Sebastian tried to write simpler music.

Sebastian and his students often gave **public** concerts in coffeehouses.

Music for a King

King Frederick the Great heard about Sebastian. The king was a talented musician, and he wanted to meet the great **composer**. So Sebastian visited the king in 1747.

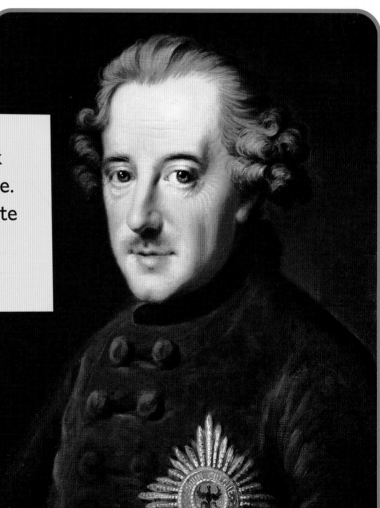

King Frederick played the flute. Sebastian wrote music for the king to play.

The king was amazed when Sebastian quickly made up such beautiful music.

The king played a simple tune. Sebastian repeated it. Then he added notes to make the music fancy. Later he **composed** a long piece using the same tune. He sent it to the king.

Sebastian's Last Years

In 1749 Sebastian began to work less. He was tired from his job. But he also had a much bigger problem. He was starting to go blind.

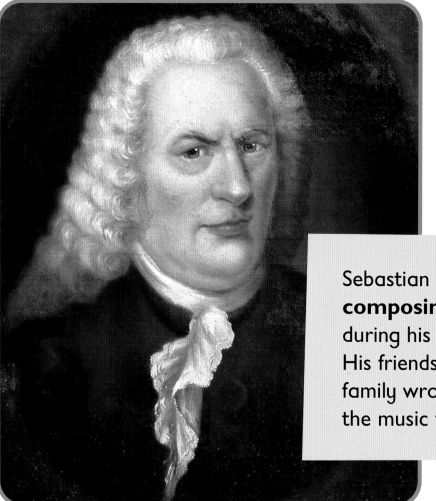

Sebastian kept **composing** during his illness. His friends and family wrote down the music for him.

Sebastian had two operations, but they did not help. His sight grew worse, and he became very sick. On July 28, 1750, Sebastian died at the age of 65. He was buried in Leipzig.

There are many statues of Sebastian in Germany. This one is in Leipzig.

JOHANN SEBASTIAN BACH

The Music Goes On

For years Sebastian was best known for his **organ** playing. People did not understand what a great **composer** he was. It took a long time for him to become famous.

The composer Felix Mendelssohn helped interest people in Sebastian's music again.

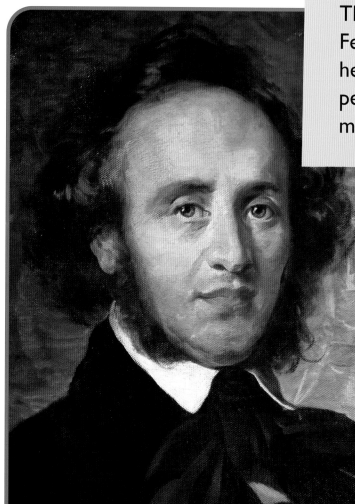

The *Voyager* recordings will play if the ships ever meet life on another planet.

Sebastian's music was **published** after he died. It is still popular today. His music has even traveled into space. The two *Voyager* ships carry recordings of three of his pieces.

Fact File

- Sebastian practiced the **organ** a lot. His little fingers grew as strong as his other fingers. This helped him play hard music more easily.

- Sebastian learned to fix organs when he was a teenager. Towns often invited him to play their organs. They asked him to suggest ways to make their instruments sound better.

- Sebastian liked to hear great **musicians** perform. He once walked a very long way to hear a famous **organist**. The trip took him four months.

- A woman poet wrote the words for some of Sebastian's pieces. This was very unusual at the time. Only men were supposed to **compose** or perform music.

Timeline

1685	Sebastian is born in Germany on March 21
1694	Sebastian's mother dies
1695	Sebastian's father dies; Sebastian moves in with his oldest brother
1700	Sebastian goes away to school
1703	Sebastian becomes a church organist
1707	Sebastian starts a new church job; he marries his cousin Maria Barbara
1708	Sebastian starts work for **Duke** Wilhelm Ernst
1717	Sebastian leaves for Prince Leopold's **court**
1720	Maria Barbara dies
1721	Sebastian marries Anna Magdalena
1723	Sebastian starts work at St. Thomas's Church in Leipzig
1747	Sebastian visits King Frederick the Great
1750	Sebastian dies on July 28

Glossary

Baroque period time in history when art, music, and buildings were very fancy

choir group of singers

compose to make up music

composer person who makes up music

court home of a ruler or other important person

duke ruler of a small part of a country

harpsichord keyboard instrument that makes sound by plucking strings inside it

keyboard row or set of keys that can be pressed to make sound

musician person who makes music

orchestra musical group that contains many different instruments

organ keyboard instrument that makes many different sounds, usually by pushing air through pipes

organist person who plays an organ

pastor person in charge of a church

patron person who gives money or support to a person or group

public open to everyone

publish have something printed so that it can be sold to other people

style way of doing things

viola instrument that looks like a violin, but is a little bit larger

Find Out More

More Books to Read

Cencetti, Greta. *Bach.* New York, N.Y.: Peter Bedrick Books, 2001.

Turner, Barrie Carson. *Johann Sebastian Bach.* North Mankato, Minn.: Chrysalis Education, 2003.

Winter, Jeanette. *Sebastian: A Book about Bach.* Chicago, Ill.: Raintree, 1999.

Places to Visit

There are many places that honor Sebastian today. These include:

Sebastian's birthplace, Eisenach, Germany
Sebastian's burial place, St. Thomas's Church, Leipzig, Germany.

In the United States, many places have festivals of Sebastian's music. These include:

Boulder, Colorado
Carmel, California
Eugene, Oregon
Philadelphia, Pennsylvania
Washington, D.C.
Winter Park, Florida.

Index